JOHN F. KENNEDY'S ASSASSINATION

ROCKS AMERICA

BY SHANNON BAKER MOORE

The Child's World
childsworld.com

Published by The Child's World®
1980 Lookout Drive • Mankato, MN 56003-1705
800-599-READ • www.childsworld.com

Photographs ©: Universal History Archive/Universal Images Group/Getty Images, cover, 1; Cecil Stoughton/dpa/picture-alliance/Newscom, 6; Houston Chronicle/AP Images, 7; AP Images, 8, 12, 16, 21, 23, 24, 28; James W. Ike Altgens/AP Images, 11; Carol M. Highsmith/The Lyda Hill Texas Collection of Photographs in Carol M. Highsmith's America Project/Library of Congress, 15; Cecil Stoughton/KRT/Newscom, 18; Ted Russell/Polaris/Newscom, 22; Linda Moon/Shutterstock Images, 26

ISBN 9781503825185
LCCN 2017959669

Printed in the United States of America
PA02376

ABOUT THE AUTHOR

Shannon Baker Moore has written many books for children and young adults. She lives with her family in St. Louis, Missouri.

TABLE OF CONTENTS

FAST FACTS

Who was John F. Kennedy?

- John F. Kennedy was born in Massachusetts on May 29, 1917.
- As a young man, Kennedy served in the navy during World War II (1939–1945).
- After serving in the war, Kennedy entered politics. He became a Democratic senator for Massachusetts in 1953. That year, he also married Jacqueline (Jackie) Bouvier.
- Kennedy became the 35th president of the United States in 1961.
- Kennedy was **assassinated** on November 22, 1963, in Dallas, Texas.

What events led to Kennedy's assassination?

- Kennedy was giving speeches across the United States in preparation for the upcoming presidential campaign that would start in 1964.
- Kennedy believed winning voters in Texas was important. He and Jackie arrived in Texas on November 21, 1963, for a two-day stay in the state.

TIMELINE

- November 22, 1963, at 11:52 a.m.: The **motorcade** carrying Kennedy and other politicians begins in downtown Dallas.
- November 22, 1963, at 12:30 p.m.: Kennedy is shot two times.
- November 22, 1963, at 1:00 p.m.: Kennedy is pronounced dead.
- November 22, 1963, at 1:50 p.m.: Lee Harvey Oswald is arrested. Authorities believe he murdered Kennedy.
- November 22, 1963, at 2:38 p.m.: Vice President Lyndon B. Johnson takes the oath of office aboard Air Force One and becomes the 36th president of the United States.
- November 24, 1963: Oswald is shot and killed by Jack Ruby.
- November 25, 1963: Kennedy is buried in Arlington National Cemetery in Virginia. Oswald's funeral is also on this day.

Chapter 1

THE ASSASSINATION

On November 22, 1963, the sun shone down on more than 150,000 people who lined the streets of downtown Dallas, Texas. Others stood in doorways or watched the street from the windows of office buildings. Schoolchildren, who had come downtown on field trips, stood with their teachers. It was an exciting day.

◀ John and Jackie Kennedy were greeted warmly when they arrived in Texas.

They hoped to catch a glimpse of President John F. Kennedy and his stylish wife, Jackie, as they traveled through the area. The famous couple sat in the back seat of a blue convertible. Texas Governor John Connally and his wife, Nellie, rode in front.

▲ Kennedy visited Fort Worth, Texas, before heading to Dallas.

Some people had told the president it might not be safe to go to Dallas. Some Dallas residents disagreed with the actions of Washington politicians. They thought these politicians were making wrong choices that were harmful to the United States. **Protesters** challenged some politicians who came to speak in Dallas. At one event, protesters hit a politician with their picket signs and spat on him.

But on that warm November day, the president and First Lady were excited to be in Dallas. They waved to cheering crowds. The gray skies from that morning had cleared to reveal a blue sky.

The president's convertible inched its way down the street. It moved slowly, at approximately 11 miles per hour (18 kmh). People shouted and cheered as they caught a glimpse of the president. Some schoolchildren waved a sign that read, "Please stop and shake our hands."[1] The sign caught Kennedy's eye. He ordered the car to stop. Children and adults crowded around the car, and Kennedy leaned out to greet them. "He shook my hand! The president shook my hand!" shouted one boy after he met the president.[2] Kennedy stopped a second time for another group of schoolchildren. Given all the crowds, no one paid much attention to the man who watched Kennedy from the sixth-floor window of the Texas School Book **Depository** on Elm Street.

◂ **Kennedy was one of the youngest presidents in U.S. history.**

At approximately 12:30 p.m., the presidential motorcade turned left onto Elm Street. From there, it was only five more minutes to the Dallas Trade Mart, where Kennedy was scheduled to have lunch and give a speech. The president's convertible passed the book depository. Suddenly, the crack of gunshots ripped through the air. Kennedy's hands flew to his neck, and blood began flowing through his fingers. Jackie leaned in, trying to help her injured husband. The crowd screamed. More shots rained down onto the scene. As Connally turned around to look at the president, he himself was shot in the back. He said, "My God, they are going to kill us all."[3] His wife held him. Although Connally was seriously injured, he eventually recovered.

Kennedy slumped onto the car's seats as another bullet hit him, this time on the right side of his head. Jackie tried to crawl out of the car. Blood covered her dress and ran down her leg.

Secret Service agent Clint Hill jumped onto the car. He had one job: protect the president and First Lady. He pushed Jackie back into the car. She crouched over the president's body. Hill threw himself over her and the president.

The limousine raced to Parkland Hospital just a few minutes away. The car pulled into the emergency room parking lot and Secret Service agents raced inside to find help for Kennedy. Hospital personnel rushed the president to a trauma room.

There, doctors frantically tried to save him, but there was nothing they could do. A Catholic priest said a final prayer for the president. At 1:00 p.m., Kennedy was pronounced dead.

▲ Secret Service agent Clint Hill ran to the president's car after Kennedy was shot.

Chapter 2

KENNEDY'S KILLER

Lee Harvey Oswald stood near the sixth-floor window at the Texas School Book Depository. For a moment he looked down at the street and saw the panic he had caused. The crowd of people were alarmed by the shooting. Kennedy's car raced down the street, away from the scene. He wondered if he had been successful in shooting the president.

◄ **Lee Harvey Oswald (center) tried and failed to become a citizen of the Soviet Union before killing Kennedy.**

Oswald stepped away from the window and shoved the rifle he used between stacks of boxes and raced to escape. He sped down the stairs and made it to the second floor without drawing suspicion. Then, a Dallas police officer spotted him and ordered him to stop.

The officer was searching the building, looking for the shooter. He had the building manager with him. The officer looked Oswald up and down before asking the manager, "Do you know this man?"[4] The manager replied that Oswald worked in the building. Oswald took deep, quiet breaths and tried to look casual. It did not occur to the police officer that an employee in the building might be the killer. The officer let him go.

Oswald walked past them, hardly believing his luck. He decided it would look less suspicious if he walked out the front door rather than trying to sneak out the back. He calmly exited the building onto Elm Street. People were running through the streets in panic. Secret Service agents, police, and reporters swarmed everywhere. A man grabbed Oswald, and for a split second, he froze. He thought he had been caught. But it was only a reporter asking where to find a telephone.

No one suspected Oswald as he escaped. He didn't own a car or know how to drive, so he fled the scene by boarding a bus. He soon switched to a cab because the streets were choked with traffic as people left to go home. Oswald eventually reached the **boarding house** where he lived in Dallas. He hurried to his room, changed his jacket, and grabbed a small gun that he owned. He slipped the gun in his jacket pocket and left. It had been less than one hour since he had shot the president.

Oswald didn't know it, but some people had seen him as he stood in the window of the Texas School Book Depository. They reported a description of him to the police. A witness to the shooting, Arnold Rowland, told police about a man he saw standing in the sixth-floor window of the depository holding a rifle. Rowland described the man as light-skinned and "rather slender" with short, dark hair, probably around 30 years old.[5] Rowland thought the man was a Secret Service agent assigned to protect the president.

After Oswald left his house, he started walking on a downtown Dallas street. Police officer J. D. Tippit was driving by and noticed Oswald. The officer stopped. He thought Oswald was acting suspicious. Tippit got out of his car and started walking toward Oswald. Oswald clutched the gun in his pocket. The metal was warm in his hand. Oswald panicked as Tippit approached. He pulled out his gun and shot Tippit four times.

Some people who witnessed the shooting quickly called the police.

Patrol cars swarmed the area, looking for Tippit's killer. Oswald snuck into a dark movie theater and tried to hide.

▲ The sixth floor of the old Texas School Book Depository has a memorial for Kennedy.

LOVED

But witnesses spotted Oswald and reported him. Soon, 15 police officers surrounded the theater. Armed officers ran inside. The theater lights came on, and a witness identified Oswald as Tippit's killer. "Well, it's all over now," said Oswald.[6] Then, he punched one officer and tried to pull his gun out of his pocket. Four officers tackled him. Oswald was taken to police headquarters for questioning. The police, Secret Service, and FBI all thought Oswald was guilty of killing Kennedy. They questioned him repeatedly, but he never confessed to murdering anyone.

Two days later, on November 24, Dallas police decided to move Oswald from police headquarters to the county jail. The police had received death threats against Oswald, and they felt they needed to move him to a more secure location. It was almost midnight as police walked Oswald down a basement hallway in the Dallas City Jail. The hall was crowded with reporters. Suddenly, a Dallas man named Jack Ruby shoved his way through the crowd. He shot Oswald three times. News cameras were running, and people saw the shooting live on TV. After the shooting, Ruby said, "I was all tore up over the president's killing. I built up a grief, and I just felt terribly sorry for Mrs. Kennedy and I didn't want to see her have to come back to Dallas for a trial."[7] Oswald died two hours later.

◂ **People in Dallas mourned Kennedy after he was killed.**

Chapter 3

LAID TO REST

After Kennedy was shot, the Secret Service feared for Vice President Lyndon B. Johnson's safety. They snuck him out of the hospital and raced him back to the airport. The car pulled up right next to Air Force One, the presidential airplane. The agents surrounded Johnson as they hurried him up the steps and into the plane. They pulled down the shades on the airplane so no one could see inside.

◀ **Lyndon B. Johnson was sworn into office by Judge Sarah T. Hughes.**

They wanted him back in Washington, DC, as soon as possible, where it would be easier to keep him safe.

Jackie was also on the plane. The presidential staff was worried about her. She was in shock. Her husband's blood was on her face, and more blood had stained her dress and tights. People asked her if she wanted to change into clean clothes. Jackie shook her head. She said, "I want the world to see what Dallas has done to my husband."[8]

Before Air Force One took off, Johnson took the oath of office as the new president of the United States. In the cabin of the airplane, Johnson stood before a federal judge. The cabin was crowded with presidential staff. His wife, Lady Bird, and Jackie stood by his side. In a somber, slow voice, Johnson repeated the words of the oath and became the 36th president.

Air Force One landed at Andrews Air Force Base near Washington, DC. The November sky was dark. Thousands of people stood near the runway, including reporters, politicians, and Air Force personnel. This time there were no shouts, cheers, or happy voices as people waited for the plane.

Kennedy's brother Robert was the **attorney general**, an important government official. He waited for the plane to land.

Then, Robert rushed onboard to find Jackie. For the next few days, during all the funeral arrangements and planning, Jackie often had Robert by her side. He was a friend and a comfort, and he loved his brother as much as Jackie did. Jackie was also glad to have her two young children, Caroline and John Jr., by her side.

As Jackie planned her husband's funeral, she wanted a special ceremony that would honor Kennedy and his place in history. The flag-draped coffin that held Kennedy's body was put in the East Room of the White House. This same room had been used for President Abraham Lincoln when he was assassinated in 1865. Jackie made sure the room was decorated exactly as it had been for Lincoln. The curtains and chandelier were draped in black fabric. The coffin rested on the same stand that had been used for Lincoln's coffin.

On November 24, Kennedy's body was moved to the Capitol Rotunda, a round room in the center of the Capitol building. More than 250,000 people came to quietly pay their respects to the president. Some people waited in line all night. Many people said the death of Kennedy was like losing a close friend or family member.

A memorial service for Kennedy was held at Washington National Cathedral. ▶

▲ More than 170 million people watched Kennedy's funeral in person and on TV.

Kennedy's funeral was held on November 25. The coffin was placed onto a wagon pulled by seven gray horses. Just as they did in Dallas, crowds lined the Washington, DC, streets. But this time there was no cheering and shouting. The crowd watched silently as the funeral march passed. Scottish bagpipers played a mournful tune as Jackie, her family, and world leaders walked from the Capitol to a cathedral for the funeral.

Leaders from almost 100 countries attended. Millions of Americans watched the service on television. After the funeral, John Jr. stood on the steps of the cathedral next to his mother. The little boy stood straight and tall. Then he raised his small hand to his brow and saluted his father one last time.

▲ The day of Kennedy's funeral was also John Jr.'s third birthday.

Chapter 4

MOVING FORWARD

Americans were shocked and saddened by Kennedy's death. The day of Kennedy's funeral, schools and businesses closed. Streets were empty as people stayed home to watch the funeral on television. Johnson declared the day of Kennedy's funeral a national day of mourning. People were especially sad to watch 34-year-old Jackie and her two young children grieving for their dead husband and father.

◀ **People lined the streets to say goodbye as Kennedy's body was moved to the Capitol Rotunda on November 24.**

For many people in the United States and around the world, Kennedy's death felt like an end to a more hopeful world. Years later, reporter Helen Thomas said, "Every president . . . had good points and bad points. But . . . you never had that sense again that we were moving forward, that we could do things."[9] One American student said, "It seemed to me that before JFK was shot, we lived in a pretty orderly country . . . we felt safe and secure—and we essentially trusted our leaders. I don't think any of us were prepared for the shock waves that resounded throughout the '60s."[10]

During his time as president, Johnson persuaded Congress to approve almost every government program Kennedy had wanted. These laws included lower taxes, money for education, and fairer conditions for black Americans. Sorrow over the assassination swayed some politicians to vote for laws Kennedy had supported.

After Kennedy's assassination, people came up with several theories as to who killed the president and why. Despite all the evidence that pointed to Oswald, not everyone was convinced he acted alone. There were some people who thought Oswald was working for a foreign government such as Cuba or Russia.

▲ The John F. Kennedy Memorial Plaza is in Dallas, Texas.

Others believed Kennedy's death was a U.S. government **conspiracy**. Johnson ordered an investigation into the assassination, and the investigation determined that Oswald was the sole killer.

Kennedy's assassination created a wave of fear and grief that spread throughout the United States. As time passed, people continued to show interest in Kennedy's assassination.

WAS JOHN F. KENNEDY'S DEATH A CONSPIRACY?

More than 50 years after Kennedy's death, many Americans still believed that multiple people were involved in his assassination.

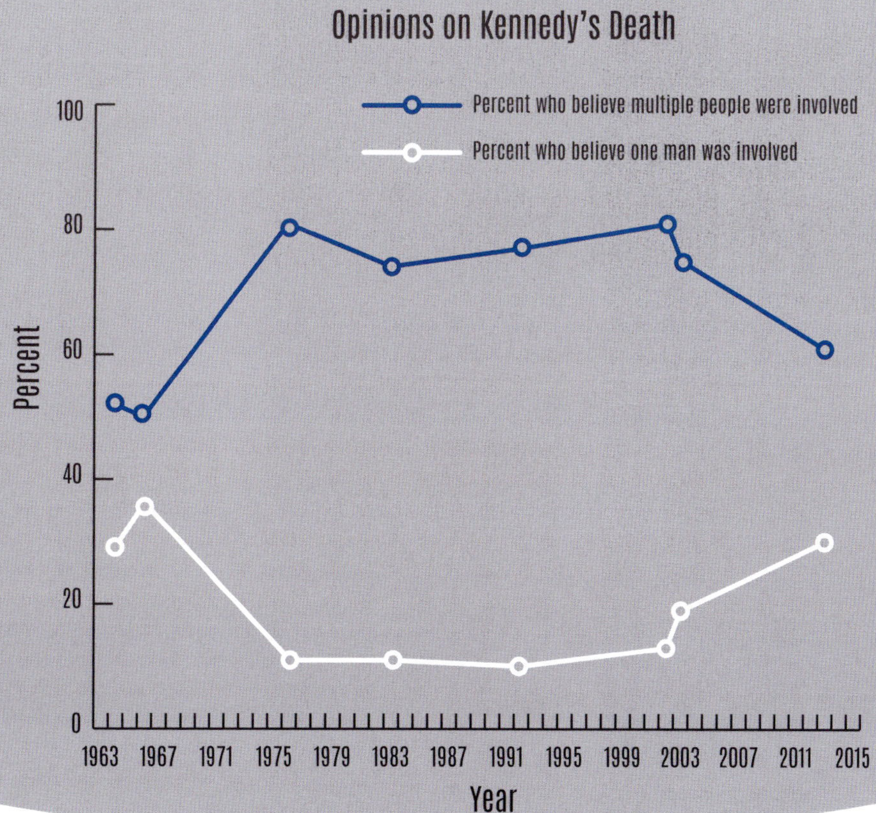

▲ Some people believe that Kennedy was a symbol of hope in the 1960s.

They demanded the government release all the information concerning Kennedy's death. Many government documents about Kennedy's assassination were marked as classified. All of the documents were required by law to be released in 2017. However, U.S. intelligence agencies recommended that President Donald Trump hold back some of the information for national security reasons. Today, many people continue to discuss Kennedy's assassination and its impact on the United States.

THINK ABOUT IT

- When he was in public, Kennedy often took time to shake hands with crowds of people. He also participated in parades. Why do you think Kennedy took time to do this?
- In 1963, television broadcasts quickly spread the news concerning Kennedy's death. What forms of media are used to spread information quickly today?
- More than 250,000 people waited in line to see Kennedy's coffin. Why do you think people did this?
- Jackie wanted Kennedy's funeral to reflect Lincoln's. Why do you think this was important to her?

GLOSSARY

assassinated (us-SAS-uh-nate-ed): If a well-known person is suddenly murdered, it is said they were assassinated. John F. Kennedy was assassinated in 1963.

attorney general (uh-TURN-ee JEN-ur-ul): The attorney general is the leader in charge of the U.S. Department of Justice who provides legal advice to the president of the United States. Robert Kennedy was the attorney general in 1963.

boarding house (BORD-ing HOUSS): A boarding house is a place, usually a family's home, where people can rent a room. Lee Harvey Oswald lived in a boarding house.

conspiracy (kuhn-SPIHR-uh-see): A conspiracy is an illegal, secret plan made by more than two people. Many Americans believe John F. Kennedy's death was a conspiracy.

depository (di-POZ-it-tor-ee): A depository is a place or building where things are stored. Lee Harvey Oswald shot John F. Kennedy from a book depository.

motorcade (MOH-tur-cade): When several vehicles move forward in a line as part of a ceremony, this is known as a motorcade. John F. Kennedy rode in a motorcade down Elm Street.

protesters (PROH-test-urz): People who act or speak up against practices are called protesters. In 1963, protesters were upset with politicians.

Secret Service (SEE-krit SUR-vis): The Secret Service is a part of the U.S. Department of Homeland Security and is responsible for protecting the president. The Secret Service agents responded quickly after John F. Kennedy was shot.

SOURCE NOTES

1. Larry Sabato. *The Kennedy Half Century: The Presidency, Assassination, and Lasting Legacy of John F. Kennedy.* New York, NY: Bloomsbury, 2013. Print. 9.

2. Ibid.

3. Jesse Greenspan. "The Other Victims of the JFK Assassination." *History.* A&E Television Networks, 18 Nov. 2013. Web. 7 Dec. 2017.

4. Larry Sabato. *The Kennedy Half Century: The Presidency, Assassination, and Lasting Legacy of John F. Kennedy.* New York, NY: Bloomsbury, 2013. Print. 11.

5. James Swanson. *End of Days: The Assassination of John F. Kennedy.* New York, NY: Harper Collins, 2013. Print. 115.

6. Larry Sabato. *The Kennedy Half Century: The Presidency, Assassination, and Lasting Legacy of John F. Kennedy.* New York, NY: Bloomsbury, 2013. Print. 19.

7. Vincent Bugliosi. *Four Days in November: The Assassination of President John F. Kennedy.* New York, NY: W. W. Norton & Co., 2007. Print. 971.

8. Larry Sabato. *The Kennedy Half Century: The Presidency, Assassination, and Lasting Legacy of John F. Kennedy.* New York, NY: Bloomsbury, 2013. Print. 14.

9. Vincent Bugliosi. *Four Days in November: The Assassination of President John F. Kennedy.* New York, NY: W. W. Norton & Co., 2007. Print. 1507.

10. Rick Hampson. "JFK's Death: People Recall Where They Heard the Fateful News." *USA Today.* USA Today, 17 Nov. 2013. Web. 7 Dec. 2017.

TO LEARN MORE

Books

Bader, Bonnie. *Who Was Jacqueline Kennedy?* New York, NY: Grosset & Dunlap, 2016.

Duffield, Katy S. *John F. Kennedy.* Mankato, MN: The Child's World, 2017.

Norwich, Grace. *I Am John F. Kennedy.* New York, NY: Scholastic, 2013.

Web Sites

Visit our Web site for links about John F. Kennedy:
childsworld.com/links

Note to Parents, Teachers, and Librarians: We routinely verify our Web links to make sure they are safe and active sites. So encourage your readers to check them out!

INDEX